Editor — Karen Barker
Language Consultant — Betty Root
Natural History Consultant — Dr Gerald Legg

Carolyn Scrace is a graduate of Brighton College of Art in England, specializing in design and illustration. She has worked in animation, advertising, and children's fiction and non-fiction. She is a major contributor to the popular *Worldwise* series and *The X-ray Picture Book* series, particularly **Amazing Animals**, **Your Body**, and **Dinosaurs**.

Betty Root was the Director of the Reading and Language Information Centre at the University of Reading in England for over twenty years. She has worked on numerous children's books, both fiction and non-fiction.

Dr Gerald Legg holds a doctorate in zoology from Manchester University in England. His current position is biologist at the Booth Museum of Natural History in Brighton, England.

David Salariya was born in Dundee, Scotland, where he studied illustration and printmaking, concentrating on book design in his post graduate year. He has designed and created many new series of children's books for publishers in the U.K. and U.S.

An SBC Book conceived, edited and designed by
The Salariya Book Company
25 Marlborough Place, Brighton BN1 1UB

First published in Great Britain in 1999 by Franklin Watts

First American edition 2000 by Franklin Watts/Children's Press
A Division of Grolier Publishing
90 Sherman Turnpike
Danbury, CT 06816

Visit Franklin Watts/Children's Press on the Internet at:
http://publishing.grolier.com

Library of Congress Cataloging-in-Publication Data

Scrace, Carolyn.
    The journey of a turtle / written and illustrated by Carolyn Scrace; created & designed by David Salariya.
        p.   cm. --- (Lifecycles)
    Includes index.
    Summary: Illustrations and simple text describe how green turtles migrate from their feeding grounds in order to lay eggs which will hatch into baby turtles.
    ISBN 0-531-14520-4 (lib. bdg)
    ISBN 0-531-15419-X (pbk)
    1. Green turtle--Migration--Juvenile literature. [1. Green turtle. 2. Turtles.] I. Salariya, David. II. Title. III. Series.
QL666.C536S38 1999
597.92--dc21
                                            98-19040
                                                CIP

AC

lifecycles

The Journey of a Turtle

Written and Illustrated by Carolyn Scrace

Created & Designed by David Salariya

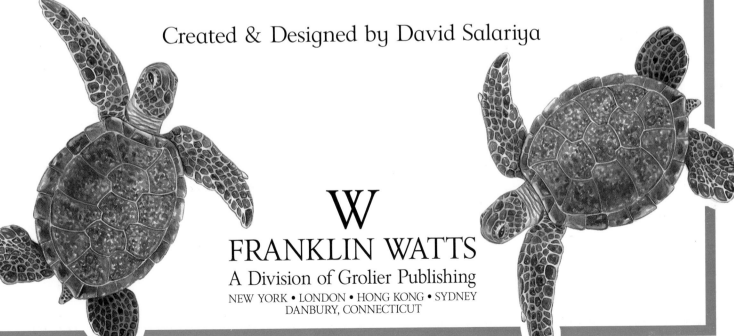

W

FRANKLIN WATTS

A Division of Grolier Publishing

NEW YORK • LONDON • HONG KONG • SYDNEY
DANBURY, CONNECTICUT

Green turtles live in warm seas.
They swim long distances
to islands in the
Atlantic and Pacific Oceans
(see map on pages 26-27).
There they lay their eggs
on sandy beaches.
Afterwards the turtles
swim home again.
Their whole journey is called
a *migration*.
In this book you can follow the
amazing migration of a green turtle.

Green turtles are covered by a large horny shell. They have two strong front flippers, which they use like paddles when they swim.

Horny shell

Strong front
flippers

Adult green turtles
eat plants such as seaweed.
They find their food in shallow water.

The turtles
leave their feeding grounds
when the weather gets colder,
and start to migrate.
They are strong swimmers.
Some turtles swim over
1,500 miles (2,500 km) on
their migration journey.

The turtles reach the breeding ground.
The female turtle waits until nightfall
then drags herself up the beach.
She uses her flippers to dig a hole
called a nesting chamber.
This is where she lays
her eggs.

Nesting chamber

The female turtle comes
onto the beach at night.
That's when the sand is cooler.
Other animals cannot see her
in the dark, so it is safer too.

The female turtle lays over 100 eggs
in the nesting chamber.
She pushes sand over the hole
to hide the eggs.

After about ten days
the turtle returns
to lay a new clutch of eggs
in another nesting chamber.
During about two months she lays
five or six clutches of eggs.

When dawn comes, the female turtle drags herself back down the beach. She swims out to sea, where the male turtle is waiting for her.

The male and
female turtle mate.

19

The sand covering the nest
protects the eggs from
the heat of the sun.
Inside the eggs,
baby turtles begin to grow.

After about seven weeks the baby turtles start to hatch. At nightfall, the baby turtles dig themselves out of the nesting hole and crawl down the beach to the ocean.

Crabs, birds, snakes, and cats will all try to eat baby turtles on land. In the ocean they can be eaten by sharks and crocodiles.

Once they reach the ocean, the baby turtles start their long journey back to the feeding ground.
The parent turtles do not wait for them and not all of the baby turtles will survive.

The parents and young turtles who do get home have completed the migration.

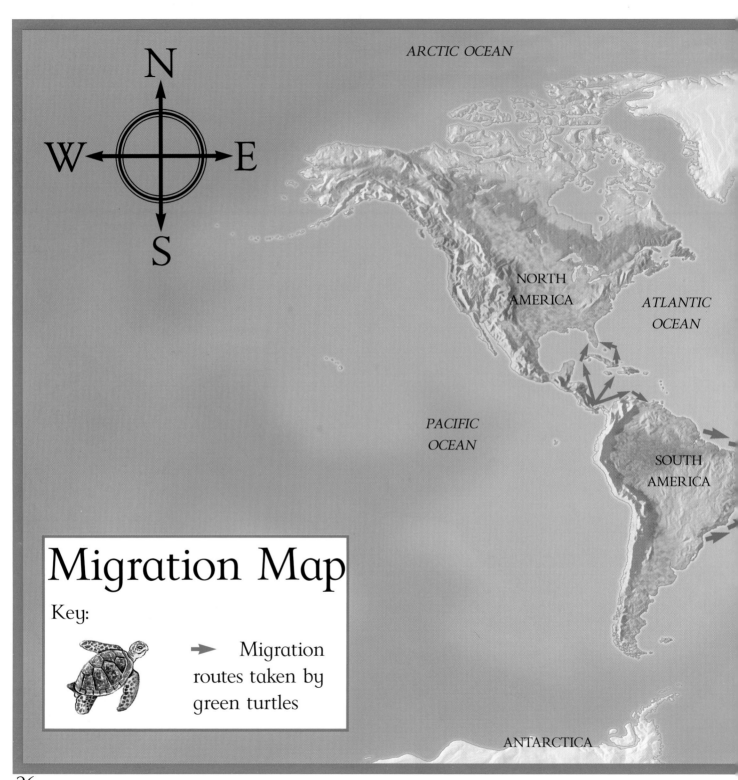

ARCTIC OCEAN

NORTH
AMERICA

ATLANTIC
OCEAN

PACIFIC
OCEAN

SOUTH
AMERICA

ANTARCTICA

Migration Map

Key:

→ Migration routes taken by green turtles

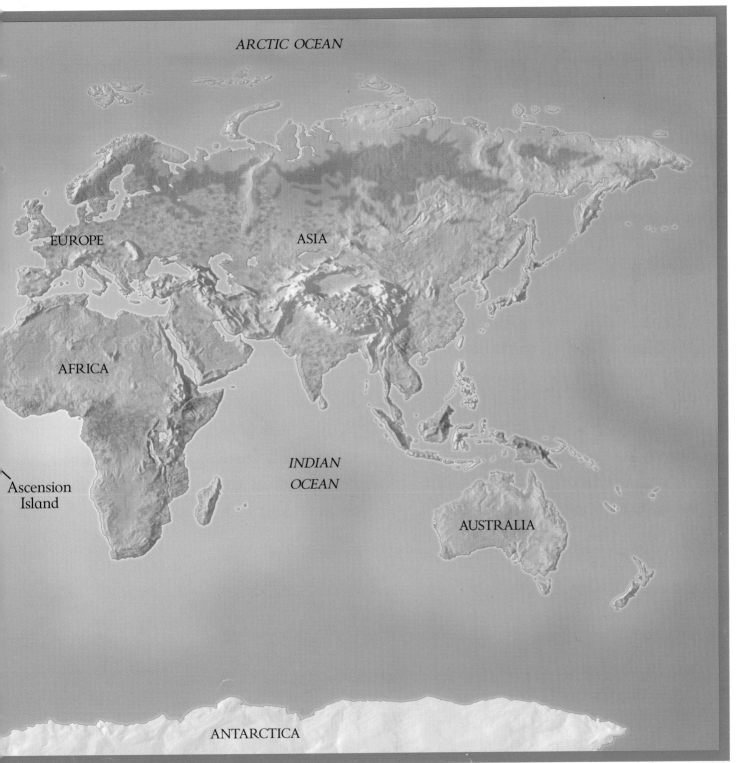

ARCTIC OCEAN

EUROPE

ASIA

AFRICA

Ascension
Island

*INDIAN
OCEAN*

AUSTRALIA

ANTARCTICA

Turtle Words

Atlantic Ocean
The huge ocean between the east coast of America and the west coasts of Europe and Africa

Clutch
A group of eggs laid by the female turtle

Dawn
The time when the sun begins to rise at the beginning of the day

Hatch
When the baby turtle breaks out of its eggshell

Mating
When a mother (female) and a father (male) join to make babies

Nesting chamber
The hole in the sand dug by the female turtle in which she lays her eggs

Nightfall
When night comes and daylight ends

Pacific Ocean
The largest and deepest of the world's oceans, stretching between the west coast of America and the eastern coast of Southeast Asia

Shallow
Water that is not very deep. Turtles find most of their food in shallow water

Shell
The hard covering of an egg that protects the growing baby turtle inside

Survive
To live through a difficult or dangerous time, like the baby turtles who are not killed and eaten on their journey

Index

Open a child's eyes to the natural world!

Each book in this series tells the amazing story of an animal's migration in the simplest possible way. Clear, colorful illustrations by Carolyn Scrace depict the different stages of the journey, and provide a starting point for discussion and further exploration.

The books also include a map showing the migration route, and a useful information section to practice reference skills.

Natural history consultant: Dr Gerald Legg

Reading consultant: Betty Root

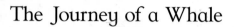

Titles in the series:

The Journey of a Whale

The Journey of a Butterfly

The Journey of a Turtle

The Journey of a Swallow

ISBN 0-531-18601-6

U.S. 3.99

A FRANKLIN WATTS BOOK